D0761517

Lingo

Akron Series in Poetry

AKRON SERIES IN POETRY
Elton Glaser, Editor

Lingo

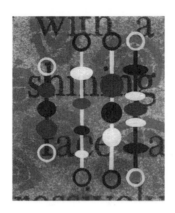

Poems by
Clare Rossini

The University of Akron Press
Akron, Ohio

[handwritten inscription:] Clare Rossini
To David,
with admiration
and gratitude for
all you've
done for
literature in
this noisy age
of ours!
Clare *[signature]*
West Hartford
7/12/06

Copyright © 2006 by Clare Rossini
All rights reserved
First Edition 2006
Manufactured in the United States of America.
10 09 08 07 06 5 4 3 2 1

All inquiries and permission requests should be addressed to the Publisher,
The University of Akron Press, 374B Bierce Library, Akron, Ohio 44325-1703.

I gratefully acknowledge the following publications in which several of these poems first appeared, some of them in slightly different versions: *Bellingham Review*, "From Grandview Terrace" (originally "South End Love Poem") and "The Roses of Hartford"; *Cascadia Review*, "Barbarian from the Midwest"; *Connecticut Review*, "To a Friend in Basque Country"; *Crab Orchard Review*, "Homage to Mister Berryman"; *Diner*, "The Unsaid"; *The Georgia Review*, "Lesson"; *The Iowa Review*, "Postmortem"; *The Kenyon Review*, "Brief History of a Sentence"; *Parthenon West*, "To the Lilac Bush," "My Mother Reads Me Lear's Alphabet," "Portuguese Bakery, Hartford," "A Hartford Collage," and "Cold Bone"; *The Texas Review*, "Eden, the Annual Exhibition," "Ultrasound," and "The Akropolis Deli" (originally "Afterlives of the Gods: Jove").

Three sections of "Gods of the South End" appeared in *Manthology: Poems of the Male Experience,* ed. Roger Weingarten and Craig Crist-Evans (University of Iowa, 2006), in slightly different forms: "The Akropolis Deli," "The Maple Café," and "South End Pizza." "Brief History of a Sentence" and "Rice County Soliloquy" appeared in *Poets of the New Century,* ed. Roger Weingarten and Richard M. Higgerson (David Godine, 2002). "Rice County Soliloquy" also appeared in *Plain Songs II,* ed. Rebecca Harrison (Black Willow Press, 2000).

Many thanks to the Bush Foundation, Carleton College, the Minnesota State Arts Board, the Connecticut Commission on the Arts, and Trinity College, all of which provided support for the writing of these poems.

I am grateful to the readers who helped these poems find their way: Robin Behn; The Brickwalk Poets, including Jim and Susan Finnegan, Paula Nelson, Charles Chase, Gray Jacobik, Marilyn Johnston, Jeff Mock, Maria Sassi, Ravi Shankar, Anne Sheffield, Jonathan Stolzenberg, and Connie Voisine; Elizabeth Macklin; the Faculty Poets of Carleton College, including Susan Jaret-McKinstry, John Ramsay, Bob Tisdale, and Chico Zimmerman; Rennie McQuilken; Carol Muske-Dukes; and my colleagues and advisees in the Vermont College MFA Creative Writing Program, especially my soul-sisters among them. Thanks to my colleagues at Trinity College for their support, especially Kat Power, and to Cynthia Merritt and Deborah Appleman, for their fellowship in the enterprise. A very special thanks to my editor Elton Glaser and to Sister Mary Carol, O.M.D, fellow traveler through the vale. Finally, to my best reader, Joseph Byrne, and our son, Francis, my gratitude and love.

LIBRARY OF CONGRESS CATALOGING-IN-PUBLICATION DATA

Rossini, Clare.
  Lingo / Clare Rossini.— 1st ed.
    p. cm. — (Akron series in poetry)
  ISBN 1-931968-29-2 (alk. paper)
  I. Title. II. Series.
  PS3568.O84725L56 2006
  811'.54—DC22

                          2005032843

The paper used in this publication meets the minimum requirements of American National Standard for Information Sciences—Permanence of Paper for Printed Library Materials, ANSI Z39.48–1984. ∞

Cover image: "Gatsby 1.7," mixed media on paper, Francis O'Shea, 2004. This piece is part of a 12-piece series based on the first chapter of *The Great Gatsby.*

Contents

for my parents, Reno and Rose Rossini

Love—is anterior to Life—
Posterior—to Death—
Initial of Creation, and
The Exponent of Earth—
Emily Dickinson

Foreword

My son's first word:
Star.

In a monosyllabic burst,
He tethered a thing

Huge and lonesome
And bright,

Made it
Locally burn.

Don't tell me the tongue's
Not a magical place.

Ain't it something?
As my German Grandma

Would've said,
How the very sounds

That in Rilke can make
The heart full,

Reshuffled, can sell
Cans of beans,

Reshuffled, can
Toughen into prayer?

Still, who'd trade "hand"
For the warm and living

Appendage, who'd
Substitute "love" for love?

No wonder
The dead don't speak.

I've been waiting
For my sweethearts of ash

To drop their stubborn
Habits of silence.

Nothing yet
But my own heart

Ticking, the tedious
Razzing of tears.

If there's *spiritus*
(As I believe),

It inhabits the space
Between words and all

Words hope to name,
That Midwest buzzing

With ions, ghosts, roots,
Griefs beyond

Mere sound.
Of the Between, I ask

That from these words
Only useful

Meanings rise.
And that music

Sashay out,
Sashay out,

I say, on my
Syllables' small feet.

.

Rice County Soliloquy

I come from Minnesota.
What do I know of the flamingo?

Its long and *s*-curved neck, its awkward flight?
If fly it does.

In my town, foreign food is pizza.
In winter and in spring, it snows.

The thought of something pink with wings
Wounds all of us, we natives

Of this land of grays and whites,
Where the template of winter was struck.

I've stood in arctic winds and felt them
Grind against my human frame.

I've looked out bleakly and borne up.
That's our way here.

Coral reefs, cabanas striped and scattered
Across beaches, blue-colored drinks:

What god made them and this place, too?
I guess he had range,

A taste for the superfluous
Exhausted by the time he shook out north.

When the going gets tough!
If the shoe fits!

Sometimes, we're surprised to find our bodies
Beneath the multiple layers,

Radiant with mammal warmth.
Dear, if the trees

Would not stand leafless
As long as they do, each rivulet of bark

Caked with frost, each forked twig scratching
A sky so blue and deep it hurts—

Busy hands! Light work!
After all, we have our lilacs,

And the balm of our May dusks will thaw
The most Protestant among us.

But the days grow short.
The light grows small.

Come those Januarial hours
When I turn the TV chitchat off

And stand on my porch, in the brittle air,
The backyard steeped in snow.

Comes something pink and winged.
Goes.

To the Lilac Bush

Flowers who have not labored
To be among us,

      Who freely ladle purple
      Into air,

            You, lilacs,

I can't smell you
Without growing young,

   This spring becoming
   Every spring

I've entered,
My senses opening

            Like mouths.

      Blossoms bordering
      On memory,

Forgive me
For pursuing liquid sound,

      I suspect
      What comes so

            Musically.

For a few days only
Your clusters fill the vacancies

Of art,
I decant

        Lilacness

Ask words to blossom
Lavenderlike

    In what hours
    They're spoken to.

My Mother Reads Me Lear's Alphabet

"A" was once an apple pie,
Pidy, widy, snidy, lidy,
Nice-insidey, apple pie!

            Mid-May,
The windows thereby open, the breeze thereby
Dispensing smells of turned earth, cow dung
Packed around my dad's tomatoes, fresh tar
Anointing the streets of the town's north end.

          This, the bouquet of spring,
          And the birds profuse.

My mother, by noon, already exhausted
By her ministry to the wash and stove,
The cracked linoleum floor.

          No time,
She'd sigh, for words not designed to get us
Washed or fed or into heaven. *Better*
Just say a prayer today.

           But to hear
Those syllables that meaning had all
But fled, delicious as the earthly stuff
That we were told to yearn away from—

          Well, my mother said,
          Bless her, always said,

Mister Lear, it'll be.

Doodads of sound!
The lord of misrule waltzing drunken
Through the napping room, the crucifix
To the wall above us
                    crooked clinging.

A Provincial's Lament

I want to write of Rome, its tarnished light.
But the sun calls my eye to our street,
Neither broad nor famous. I want
To write of anything but you, my maple.
We're friends, of course, we know one another
As only a tree and a woman can.
But alleys cooled by palms, the frayed ends
Of big stone shapes that the centuries
Have run roughshod over: these are what
The hour seems to call for, not the silos
That I behold from my window, looking north.
To hold for awhile the grail of elsewhere!
The cheap pensione, the ruin of a bed
Where I once lay and closed my eyes to see
Not the moon of Rome but our own shy thing,
Homely, homeless in makeshift fields of stars.

The Roaring

St. Paul Zoo, 1963

It beat against my head,
Washed across the popcorn wagon, swallowed
Whole the fountain throwing its water
Carelessly up.

          The seals barked in their pool.
The monkeys seemed human as ever.
One combed and combed the fur of its beloved,
Stopping to pick things out. Nits? Or crumbs?

Just when I thought that I was safe, the roaring
Came again, full-throated, gnawing, huge.

When my brothers said, *Let's find the lion!*
I said that I would not, wanting nothing
Of a muscled litheness pacing a tiny,
Hosed-down space, with raw meat scattered on the floor.

Now, if I could make a sound like that, ask wind
To carry its tide of drastic music
And fill the wondering ear with all
The heart already knows, I would.

Eden, the Annual Exhibition

Painted flats,
Wood and plaster figures, all of them
Life-size,

You bet,
Said the guy in the ticket booth,
Like nothin' nowhere else you've seen.

Look, a father would say to his son,
There's the Tree of Knowledge,
And pointed to the famous apple's
Varnished red.

Don't touch!
The hand-printed sign above said,
Rigged with alarms!

Beneath the tree, why,
It was our friend the snake,
A blithe confection of tin and paint,
A tape somewhere inside him rasping,
Want to be a god, a god, a god?

His pink mechanical tongue
Slid in and out. His eyes looked blank
With joy at the thought
Of our impending demotion.

And Adam and Eve,
Their plaster figures chipped
From years of storage in the town garage,

Their faces,
Sculpted winters ago
By a farmer with time on his hands—

Adam bawling to the sky, Eve
Looking straight ahead, as if to the fields where
Our plows were raising the spring's
Showers of dust.

Was she making a *to-do* list in her head?
Get some food on the table. Mother
A kid or two. Die.

Above the pair, bumbling down a wire,
It was God Almighty. I think they did
A good job with God.

He was a mist
Troubled by flashes of light, thunder
Manufactured somewhere on site—
You could hear the generator's hum.

I itched to know that awkward contraption,
And every year would raise a child's hand
Toward what looked to be
God's shifting face.

A pulley whined.
The mist whistled up its rope, vanished
In a heaven of plywood clouds.

Flashback

Stalled by your pint-sized coffin heaped with the flowers
That we'd brought to your death, we waited.
The priest closed his book, looked up, gently said,
Let go, and the balloons we'd held in our hands
Veered skyward with what seemed a strange joy.

Bright for awhile, they grew gray and distant,
Knocking against the high, abstract clouds. . . .

I've found again the equanimity
Beloved of the living, removed
From the chokehold of grief, sleeping although
September's skittish stars are falling.

                               Then
The light shifts, making a room go strange.
Then I gaze on the brief expanse of my own
Son's body, struck heavily by sleep,

And I'm stumbling again toward your small
Stilled body, wrenching words into prayer,

As if prayer could be heard above the din
Of your precocious silence.

In memory of my nephew, JMR (1999-2001)

County Road 42

The sheep was soiled gray, fat,
Gnawing a hillside in slanted light.

The grass so green it burned.
Gone then, in heat and dust behind.

I felt nothing. I was going fast,
My speed, my sweet bouquet.

A girl in flowered dress appeared,
Flashed by. A brook sprawled

Among rocks. One looked
At me, as greened and cleft as a heart

Might be, but just a rock,
Just a rock. We fell in love,

The road and I. The road, genius
Of the flat and straight,

The curve, the hill that slowly
Lifted me toward lonesome sky.

But nothing out there *meant,*
Not sheep nor rock nor girl

In flowered dress. In retrospect,
That's what I liked about this

Long drive-dream of mine:
Nothing meant.

The Diagrammer of Sentences

for my father

Beneath the kitchen's halo of fluorescence
I stood shyly at your side,
The pen in your big freckled fist
Filleting sentence after sentence,

Whether compound or not,
With all manner of tenses shivering,
And the phrase singled out, and the absolute exposed.

Music from the stove a few feet away,
My mother humming, pot lids clanking,

Above and below and around, cries and laughter—

Ten of us crammed into that bungalow
Braced against the winter riding in
From the frost-shorn fields.

Find the subject,
You said to me, *That's the proper start—*

Subject or object, which was I?

And then the predicate, with its verb—

To sing, to pray, to think, to be,
How could words contain such festering?

"To modify," you said, *Is to shape, to fix qualities to—*

Word-love infecting the air we breathed,
The dictionary presiding at supper
Night after night, a Prospero's book
Of roots and derivations,

And scraps of paper fluttering on the walls,
Poems, proscriptions, prayers,
Some in foreign tongues:

> *In medio stat virtue.*

> *In bocca chiusa,*
> *Non ci entra mosche.*

> *Character is all.*

Wind banged the house-side
As you looked sideways up, your eyes
Behind your thick black glasses
Studying my face.

Want to try? you asked, then turned back
To the blank white universe
Your hand held in place, printing a sentence there
With a flourish.

Did I take the pen,
Scatter your words on my own diagram's broken,
Sideways tree?

I remember the sentence
You made for me:

> *Gladly the man and his daughter walked up the hill.*

Local Color

What the light out here'll do.

Make you see clearly, without shirking,
The too-long winter, too-wet spring,
Your fate tethered to a cloud's inclination
To loiter or not,
To fritter a shower or not on your corn.

But nights, some nights,
The air grows soft, almost Parisian.

It calls young men to their pickups
To circle the Mega-Store lot,
Its apparition of high-school girls.

They shatter the pink spectrum.
Stiff in new jeans, teetering
On high-heeled shoes, those girls so young,
So unreal that, looking,
You feel the sweet artificial flutter
Of your own passing life. . . .

The bars close at one.
The fish in the river sleep suspended,
Every last nomadic
Chevy home.

Father O.

Eyes arrogating the ceiling,
Father O'Ryan,
Man o' the cloth, spoke:

> *Of late, you girls be*
> *looking like this—*

With his hands,
Sketching a womanly shape
Like some
Disfigurement of air.

> *And now*

(Eyes moving sadly
Over the rows,
Sunlight breaking
On our heads its vacant
Columns of dust)

> *There be thoughts,*
> *My children,* words
> *In your head, and your soul*
> *'Tis ash 'til you confess.*

Beneath the rheumy
Eyes of the good
Father, engulfed
In the flames of innocence,
I thought

> *What words could those be?*

The perilous equals
Of those that in Mass
Catapulted human bread
To the flesh of godhood—

Hic est corpus meum.

Looking furtively down
To my dark
Green uniform, wherein
The carnal byways that grace
Couldn't teach—

Hic est corpus meum.

The air ghosting with words,
Ripe for the plucking.

Homage to Mister Berryman

Maybe you and I passed one day
Beneath the torpid elms of the U,
You hunkering toward class, sun aslant
On your glasses;

I, AWOL from girl's school,
A stack of dittoed manifestoes purpling my hands
As I ran to meet the radical crew
Who struck when the war got hot.

Riding home on the bus, I opened
Your book of songs, flushing
As they assailed my ear.

The scrumptious iambic, my only tune
Until your weird polyphony, Mr. B.,
Brought me eye to eye, nay,
Gut to gut with chasms.

Not grace, but saliva;
Not wisdom, but ironic surmise
Brokered by all-night drunks that broached
The scat of blue revelation:

I staggered with you
Line after line,
Not wanting your life but your chutzpah.

O days of our final innocence,
Crowds singing in the streets,
The naked boys and girls among us wreathed
With hallucinogenic flowers!

And you, my insurgent Muse,
I snuck your book into chapel.
Your songs undid the truss
Of my too-decent verses,

Your music moving into me, a river
Of raucous sheen and dangerous bends.
How could you resist?

Your body splayed on the rocks.
My adolescence blazing out.
Our boys bombing Cambodia to kingdom come.

Self-Portrait in Midwestern Light

I'm more pig than cow.
Pigs, you know, are social beings.

Hock to hock they stand.
Tender ears and tails like sprigs:

They're some concoction, pigs, and feeling
Happiness, seem to dance

On tiny hooves,
Raising dust on barn-mud floors.

Some days, I brace for emptiness,
Bear the weight of all that sky.

I'm akin to cow then, know the amble
To the hill-brow,

The long view, the studied blink.
Thinkers, cows are; grievers, seem.

Pigs don't roam. Find a pen
And call it home, *chez famille,* that's pig!

Have you not, pig, known times
No pen could balm you?

And you, cow, left your thoughts
Beneath your trough

And given unto love
Your spotted hide?

The barn resounds with cries
Of pigs and cows

And dark of night. Times I seem
The dark of night,

The wide and deep of it, and lie
Upon my bed as though

There nothing be
But bed and night, the wide, the deep.

So the Story Goes

In the back row of the boys' chorus
Imported by Sister Rose Immacula
For the Academy's spring show,
You,

Your face washed pale
By the genes of your Irish grandmas,
Your mouth darkly open,
Emitting its song.

And I
Knew even then (so the story goes)
That the cosmic syntax some call Fate
Would bring us together.

Therefore,
In a cabin north of Bemidji,
A bare bulb dangling above us
Like a low-watt apostrophe,

We contracted
As two words might and do,
The "we" and "are" of us
Merging to a "we're,"

Sheets thrown back, mallard
In the duck-print tacked to the wall
Assuming toward its own
Swamplit heaven....

Only later to learn the joys
Of mere conjunction, which links
Rather than fuses, couples
Rather than stews,

As tonight, you and me,
Hun, and the old porch light
And the hammock,
And the cricket in the grass,

Its song whittling away the hours
And then the night,
And the night whittling away the summer,
And then the years.

The Unsaid

It stands in the living room's middle, oh,
About coffee-table size.
Seems anyone could see it.

But it's only we who can,
Who built the thing
Of private forays into truth,
Internal storms that brewed, veered, vanished
Without announcement.

It's our little monument,
Rather dark and spare.

Once or twice, I've yelled, *Let's lift*
This goddammed thing and throw it out. Stop
Vacuuming around it; cut it off
From the wariness it loves.

You've gone on reading, feet propped on its edge,
And I know I didn't speak
Aloud, again.

It's a collectible, it's awfully us,
This Spartan prop designed
For a domestic space. I've titled it
Black Cube with Tears Inside.

What do you think? What's inside you?
Forgive me for asking, forgive me for not
Asking sooner.

Sometimes I think we could point, say
Look at that, won't you?
And laugh, and it would disappear.

Just like that, love, just like that.

An Olde Complaynt

The mind, rife
With its instinctive scowl.

Listen to it extemporize
On the humdrum of the heartbeat:

Thud thud thud, it says with a snicker.
Thud thud thud.

The heart, the door
That opens and opens unto itself.

Have you tried to make your way through
In the spell of its little griefs?

Mine badger me all spring,
And in the fall, grow obdurate.

The body, paltry welling of flesh,
Plodding on through time. On and on,

On and on,
The night wind,

Roiling the curtains at the window,
Felling the last of the leaves.

Prayer of Sorts

The nothingness you emanate,
The grand reserve
You're shawled up in, leaves us both
In the nether,

For which, don't get me wrong,
I've longed at times,
Fantasizing me
Bride of the Ineffable,
Call him night, mist, the genial
Zero himself.

Yet somehow as it comes to this, our—
How to say it?—

"Relation"—

What do you seem? A shade
Vanished up the path, the path itself
Rolling up,
And the woods eating all.

I stew over your correspondences
Day and night, I finger your signs.
Were they faked?

Are *you?*

As it is, we walk on wires
Strung above vacuums. As it is, all words
Are yoked to the mute.

Let me put it this way:
The window frames a cumulus drifting.

Don't make me
Speak to clouds.

Caterpillar on Lilac Bush

Woozy from days
Of chewing leaves,
He hooks to a twig, secretes
His own novitiate.

Grows perfectly still,
Not a thing but a patience,
His breathing spiracles,
Half-blind head
Dissolved to a heave and slosh,
A cloistered
Sea of glitter.

To be a species
Of Void, alive again
In the basement of being,
Not a thing
Anymore but a word,
Sign, stab at
Lightwardness—!

But this woolly,
Much too busy
To dawdle in the dim,
His huge, disjointed eyes,
Dainty thorax,
Loopy tongue,
A cubist scramble glimpsed
Through the pupal shell
Gleaming now, clear
As spittle.

When, self-split,
He crawls out
Damp on the twig, antennae
Quizzical in morning's
Canyons of light,

What word can spell
The fear of wings
Opening for the first time?

Souvenir

The week before you died, we climbed the streets
Of an ancient town, lost among stone walls
And sudden spillages of flowers.

Just beyond the main piazza, a road
Curved up, disappearing in dusk's rustic air.
Its cobbles bore the shade of cypress trees
And, from a somewhere-setting sun, roughed-beamed gold.

Not on the map, I said, nose to my Michelin.
Beautiful, you said. I took the picture.

Now, in the photo store's chill fluorescence,
I rifle through the glossy hours we had—
Walls, geraniums, a fresco's crumbled blues.

Oh it's
          you, hand up, waving, body blurred,
Your dear face completely out of focus.

Behind, what the camera's neutral eye
Chose for clarity, photons of evening light
Searing the film's suspended grains, honing

The light-and-shade road, which you, your joy
Incarnate still, chose to call *beautiful.*

In memory of my brother, RDR (1948-2001)

Ultrasound

Today on the screen we saw you,
Cloud of unknowing, cellular snowstorm
All white and gray, your spine a pearl tiara
Sunk in your back.

You lifted one gauzy hand to your mouth. We watched,
Unnerved to have caught you like that,
In your dressing room,
Busy with your arrayment.

No getting around it:
You're among the numbered, the blooded and the fleshed.

Soon you'll know the great divide
That yawns away from all sides of the body.

Of course, you'll howl. That's your business, to protest.
Then to find a way to colonize the vacuum,
Doll it up with a god, a Kantian category,
A wall of love,

While the hours pass by,
The hours we're stuck in like flies,
The hours we drift through like music,
The wide silvery ones, the sharp cold ones,
The dense black ones, which are all some ever get:

You'll see what griefs
We concoct for one another; our tools are
Famously refined.

Your days await you. Your years, I hope,
Lie folded, stacked, scented with mud and flowers.

I said flowers,
Yes. One day we'll sit on a hill,
And I'll weave you a little crown.

Meanwhile, sweet Huck,
In your lazy tropical afternoons,
Knit a lung, carve a thumbnail,
Conjure a face.

Nocturne

Fresh-born, pink, curled
In the crib at the foot

Of my parents' double,
The Midwest of mine

Damp with its June,
Did I intuit the vastness

Of our human
Holdings of dark?

My eyes too new for sight,
I was

All ear, imbibing
The fan shushing the dresser

The shade's
Slap-slap on the sill.

And did then
Another sound open

In that infinite
And breezeless space?

My mother's voice,
A slow, ornate flowering

Speaking to my father
Lying next to her

Of the wash, oh
The piles of it today, those boys

Sure go through socks,
And Henry down the street

Stealing Graber's apples,
And the second cousin

Calling
(Isn't it something?)

All the way from Iowa.
And my father's Yes, yes,

Drowsy in reply,
Each syllable warming

My auricles, clattering through
The bony halls of the cochlea

Sinking at last
In the brain's fresh plush.

Species music!
And the crickets

Through the windows coming in
With their own

Folk-sounds,
Ching-a-ching, ching-a-ching.

Midword

Pent within the radiant
Metal skin of a DC-10,

In flight from one
Life to another,

I stare out a scratched
Plexiglas porthole

To my Midwest,
Its twilight coming on.

Below, through miles
Of cloudless air,

A freeway cloverleaf
Glitters like a brooch.

Earth, my one and only, dogged

By a moon's obsessive ebb,
Sweet planet

Of my youth and childhood,
Where's home?

Out of the depths, a voice:

Huffy Henry hid   the day

From the wrinkled vale
Of my hippocampus,

Memory-room of the brain,
Berryman's fractured

Voice and nimble-hearted
Music hauled until

> *Hard on the land wears the strong sea*
> *And empty grows every bed.*

No daughter of Mnemosyne, I.
"My mind's a sieve,"

I'm wont to say.
But hey,

    I'm on a roll,

And so to the plane's
Blinking wing I give

Mister Justice's "Ode to Yellow,"
(All of it)

Miss Bishop's "Moose,"
(The start)

Tail end of Whitman's
Baggy song,

    how goes it?

> *If you want me again look for me under your boot-soles.*

A pipe, I am, a vassal
Of music, assigned

To Seat ll-A, moving
West to east

Above the continent,
In the vacuity once

        deigned God's.

The flight attendant
Comes by for trash.

The captain's voice
Announces our descent.

I turn back to my fertile window
And, with brave Jane, choose

        "the flashboat!

                work,

                        the starry waters"

As into my lookout
The light-

Studded spines of tall buildings
Slowly rise into view.

II

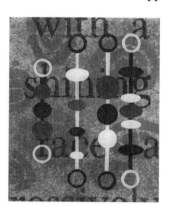

Portuguese Bakery, Hartford

A wedding cake fills the window,
Rosettes barnacled to the sides,
Dimpled ribbons wreathing the tiers,
Each pillared up and stippled
With pearl-drop flowers.

Nothing random here, nothing
Real—
Ephemera frilled on solid pasteboard.

But what a vision.
Decked out, flirting with overkill, and look
What the sign says:

"Baked on the premises."

Right here on earth!
Give enough notice, you could
Have your fiction and eat it, too,
Its fabulous shapes
Melting on your tongue like sugar and lard.

Could the real cake
Still warm from the oven,
Frosted, sliced, presented on glass plate—
Could *that* cake ever live up to this,
Its perfected effigy? I shrug

My heavy purse back onto
My shoulder, take a step
Closer to the window,
The March wind pawing my face,

Hordes of litter skittering through
The vacant lot next door.
I'm going to stop thinking awhile.
Going to stand here and allow
This audacious baked rival
To size *me* up, to take a private
Estimation of my
Human-thingness.

And when it's had enough of me,
I'll have more to say.

Heat Not Included

A realtor hounds us.

Look, she says, you could have
A roof of your own, square footages, views,
A master suite to keep away the destitute
Desires that gnaw at 3 A.M.

I like to be so gnawed.
To rise and walk upon a floor consigned
To someone else's bank. To lock the door on space
Housing a rented dark.

Below, the purgatory
Of Unit One. Their squabbles rise like steam. Their heaven
Is our earth and we've become
Their deities, padding in slippers through realms of carpeted ether,
Making our theophanies
When we go out to fetch the mail.

There's a couch that we call "ours" here,
A slew of chairs. A painting we love
For its hostel of light. A box that held a daughter's ashes, photographs
We call dear.

And this body, my portable house—
Who owns it? Me, I'd say,
If I hadn't wakened last night to see my hand
Like a five-ped splayed on the pillow, so numb with sleep it seemed
A dream's appendage.

This morning, plumbing a closet's deep space, I find a negligé
Draped on a hanger, the molting
Of a former tenant, kindred spirit.

I tried it on and it fits fine, this frail skin, a hide
Of almost-air.

The Prince of Nix

Tongue crease of the *n* sound,
Warm, wet, fluttery emptiness
Of the *o,* and you've made a word
As heady as that first
Postpartum intake of air. *No*
And the spoon of mushed carrots withdraws,
The little blue coat
Vanishes to its closet-dim.

How casually the Prince of Nix
Waves off the kiss of an aunty,
As if aunties and kisses grew on trees.

Light and dark, sea and land, fish and fowl,
No and *yes*:

              it's the *nay* that most
Becomes us, think of our forebears
Job and Medea, Gandhi and Lear. And times,
You've got to take the *via negativa*
To make friends with the light.
Mayo on that beef, sir?
Shall we go to war?

            No thanks!
Say it, kid, your *nay* or *uh-uh,*
Nope, no way and no how.

            Hey!
You've grabbed a glass trinket
I carelessly left on the table
And are staggering out of reach.

Little man, how small you seem
As you clutch your trophy to your breast
And shake your head ferociously
West, then east.

from Gods of the South End

1. The Maple Café

In the polyglot
Unmelted pot of Hartford's South End,
The grocers' shelves sag
With feta and icons, rices and beans,
Irish tea, plum tomatoes, plantains, collard greens,
Something for everyone,
Except maybe the gods,

Who, bored stiff by Olympian views, have arrived
To while away a century or two
In the new world, so-called.
They've got themselves jobs and houses,
They pay taxes and union dues. All but Cupid,

Who lives with Venus
In one of those bungalows on Freeman Street,
Still, forever, mama's boy.

Get a job, Cupie, she scolds. *I'll buy the suit.*

The days come and go, and he's still rolling his rosy
Dollop of flesh out of bed
At noon. A mug of ambrosia-latté in one hand,
He yawns, flips on the PC:

"Junctions of Love," "Macho-Matches," "Heart-throb, Inc.,"
All the dot-coms where the lonely post
Their photos and fetishes.

What's left for a minor deity
Who once brought one and one together

With an arrow's stinging buss? Poor Cupid. He's feeling
Awfully low-tech.

Thank goodness
There's always something going on
At the Maple Café,

Kathleen wiping the bar down, Miguel chalking up a cue.
Cupid loves the smell of the place, sweaty, smoky,
Vaguely secretional. His vinyl stool waiting.
Shirley, too, with her chronic sass
And festive cleavage.

Cupie, baby, she croons, tilting up
Her bright rouged cheek, swamping him
In flowery perfume.

Psyche, she ain't. But he's tired of that old grief,
And when Shirley invites him
To her small flat on Fairfield Ave.,

When she lies down among her country doodads
And lace-crazed pillows,
Cupid's ready for love
Made in America
Where the coupling's as diverse as democracy can be,

Look at this pair,
Shirley O'Reilly, Irish-Italian-Puerto Rican,
Cashier at the Worn-a-Bit Shoppe,

And Cupid, Son of Eros, the splurge
That begot a universe.

2. South End Pizza

There's an air of damaged goods
About this guy, he's got the rueful ways
Of a '60s philosophy-major burnout from Berkeley.

Who wouldn't, who'd been dumped
From the clouds by his own mother,
Irate she'd born a lame son?

Crowding his joint's patched banquettes,
The local Napolatini watch *Maestro Vulcan,*

Si,
A true *pizzaiolo:*

One bite of his pie, they say, and again
You're hearing goat bells
On the pale cliffs of Capri.

 Ecco-la!
The god throws a dervish of dough in the air,
Catches it in a floury cloud
That settles on his fist. Spreads the sauce famous
As far as New Haven, sprinkles his cheese.

As he shovels it into the oven, toward the fire's
Ravishing id,
There you are, sweetheart,
He croons to the flames.

A strange thing to love
An element, yes. Stranger still, Vulcan would tell you,
To love only the mind

Like that doll-boy Apollo, a god's god
With his six-pack abs and brain festooned
With the odds and ends of Western Civ.

Even thought burns, he tells the guys. *Even soul.*

He limps to the oven,
Retrieves a round of crust perfected
By the golden mean of cheese.

Two-ninety Grandview, Vulcan barks,
And the delivery guy (are those wings on his feet?)
Grabs the box, hustles out
The smoke-blackened door.

3. The Akropolis Market

Sky-god, Lord of the Oak,
Overseer of thunderbolt and rain
Has taken up the dentist's trade
In an office behind the Akropolis
Market on Maple.

Above the chatter of Trinity profs
Getting their daily gyros,
The piquant whine of old Doc's drill.

It's not lightning, old Doc says, but, *Hell,*
Whirring in his hand, it gives him something
Of the old thrill.

Open wide! he bellows to his patient,
Open wide!

And bends the elbowed lamp to excoriate
The human mouth with light.

It's a way to kill the infinite
Afternoons, tinkering away in a damp,
Decaying universe
Of miniature tragedies.

And he's good, Doc is,
He's got a loyal following, despite his weakness
For starting in before the Novocain
Takes hold.

He probes the gums' pink, forgiving flesh.
There, is it?

Hours later, sunk in an obese
Leather lounger, the frail stem of his martini
Balled in his fist,
Jove replays the scene:

That pretty little Classics major
Twitching in his chair, her sudden, garbled cry—

Well, it's something for an old god
On a spring night,
His blood-spotted tunic
Soaking in the sink, and Juno—

Damn her!—out again
With some demoted nymph or mortal boy.

4. Bellissima Hair Design

She's waiting by her pump-up chair,
Her Botticellian shape
Broad beneath her sea-blue caftan,
The waves of hair that lave her shoulders,
Clearly bleached.

Venus looks you over, head to toe.
A wash and set, she says. *Hun, that's what you need.*

Snaps her fingers. A trinity of girls—
All named Grace, in flowered shifts—appear
With bins of curlers, a plastic cape.

In no time at all, your head's a maze of tubes
No bigger than a pinky,
Each hair-chunk stiff and wound into the sweet
Viscosity of setting gel.

Under the dryer, as Grace Number Two
Paints your toes, you drift,
Rising hot, star-bright,
Ravishing the dawn's pastel clouds. . . .

Comb out time! Venus sings.

She mousses and fluffs
'Til you're as bouffant as a cumulus,
Each curl as tight as those that coifed
The fabled columns of Corinth.

That boy'll call tonight—
Venus' voice floats out from somewhere behind.
You turn, saying
How do you know?

But she's gone, vanished whole in a cloud
Of extra-firm-hold spray.

Writer's Rock

To come by the knowledge you have not
You must go by the way that you know not.
            John of the Cross

I wake up knowing
What life's about, I'm sure
I've got it down,

And when I look in the mirror,
It returns the smile
Of an eighteenth-century progressive,
Unalarmed by the shadows
In the faded silver, the long, deep
Crack in the glass.

Then this flecked weight catches my eye,
This chipped basalt hunk
That made its way, who knows how,
From mountain or sea
To the park down the street,

Crying a stone's cry
Until I picked it up and carried it home.

Taking in its round gray face
As I have all morning
(The plug-in teapot steaming and spitting,
The radiator knocking
Like a soul in distress), I feel a veil
Drop again,

Sunlight at the window
Breaking in and in.

Cold Bone

I have one cold bone
In my body, cantankerous
Bone that knows how easily the skin
Breaks and the heart is doused of its beating.

Wise bone, crude bone, bone
Foreign to love and to the uprising
Of such as the tulips out my window, all at once
They've appeared, smacking of red.

When the fall announces all manner
Of grandiose departures, my bone of frost
Remains aloof. And at 3 A.M., when the news
Of war flounders into
My tiny bedside radio, this sharp-toothed
Clavicle or humerus, shiftless radius or scapula, has the nerve—
The nerve!
To ever so lightly shine.

Is this the fallout
Of the mess we made in Eden, golden ages ago?
Else why should the moon out my window tonight
Torch the neighbor's lonely lilac
While beneath the very same moon, poker-faced
And brilliant as a strobe, the children of Baghdad are taken
By the bombs' relentless flowering?

Tibia or femur, tiny jealous bone of the foot,
I'd wrap you if I could in my old green sweater,
The one that staves off the shivers that come
Even in the sour heat of July.

You cherish your frost. Fend off feeling
What the children of Baghdad feel tonight, their old,
Old world breaking around them
Like a toy.

Barbarian from the Midwest

I fill your antique parlor, Yank,
Your dainty colonial chair,
Both too small
For my shifting and hemming.

Serving me cake, your hand trembles.

I've done it again.
Said too much,
Spoken too loud or soon.

How to refine a self who loved
The pigs she grew up near,
Their swill, their runts
And mud-packed thighs?

You don't know what it's like
To feel wind breaking on your body
As if you're the first standing thing
Since the light-gnawed flats of Alberta.

I'm wintry yet.

Your landscapes balm me, Yank,
These reams of hills
And steepled clouds. Even your china
Is picturesque, painted with lakes
And rills and thin
Enough to see me through,
To make of me a dim impression.

Does it wear on you,
My chronic cheer?
It's a strategy we use back there
To keep the bald horizon at bay.

I've put in my time, Yank,
Years of servitude
To the large and empty.

Lesson

The truck has lost its wheel. Too cheap
To last, I should've known it
The moment he fell in love with it
As it hung from its drugstore rack,
A fetal pickup wombed in a shiny plastic bubble,
Red-hot lightning stripes
Sizzling down its sides.

Such trucks do not last.
Such trucks intone the sharp facts
Of mortality, and now my son is over his head
In misery, practicing the old-fashioned
Human habit of grief.

Use your words, I remind
As he lifts the truck, his cheeks crisscrossed
With the glossy paths of tears.
Broken, I say. *The truck is broken, sweet.*
The sky is falling, your heart is blue.

That time of year thou mayst in me behold
When yellow leaves, or none, or few do hang:
To say it doesn't change a thing.
But sometimes, saying makes things true.

Duet in Blue-Black

The plumber clanks down
The cellar stairs, his flashlight
Squandering light
On joists floured with dust.

The furnace has been silent all morning,
And though it's April—
Blue-smooched April!—

The cold presses in.

Upstairs, I foist myself
Cautiously into the first person,
My words on the screen like a dusting
Of late-winter snow.

A voice calls from my
Bad-lit down-under,
Home to my gravity—

    Miss, where's the shut-off valve?

Down again, until I see
His face, smeared with grease, shining
Beatifically beneath a bare bulb.

    The shut-off valve? I ask,

Thinking, where's my own?

If I could wrench it open, the pent steam
Radiating up and out until I clanged
Again with music—

By the washtubs, I say.

My mentor nods and vanishes.

Out the kitchen window, I see
Daffodils, their yellow rising raucous
In the garden's dirty cloister.

We all have work to do.

Click, click, click:
My fingers on gray plastic keys
Tap out one pale line, another.

Clunk, clunk, clunk
From the basement below, then
The sheer weep of saw.

Meditation at a Stop Sign

Streaming across the intersection,
My headlights fix on the petal-daubed branches

Of a small tree. Apple is it, or pear?
Pale pink the flowers look in my lights,

Staunch enough to lift me
Into the tenderness of an urban spring dusk.

From the radio on the dash, the news
That nature's in a bad way, butterflies falling

From the shirrings of clouds, all the lovely
Doodads of earth losing their gumption.

What're they worth, anyhow? some say.
That would be the dark in us speaking.

A honk from behind. I glance in my mirror:
Some guy shakes his fist. I shake mine back,

Hit the pedal, and barrel my rusting wagon
Across the intersection, passing the tree,

Which floods the car momentarily
With its reckless perfume.

Gone then, another blooded thing absorbed
Into the shivering smear of our small city.

But I'm surprised how pink those blossoms
Hold in my mind, even now, how steady.

A Hartford Collage

Should include a stretch or two
Of canvas bare as the vacant lots
Where the houses of crack once stood;

A slew of bright stripes
For the ponchos in *El Serape*'s windows,
Home to the best tortillas in town.

Gold leaf, just a tad, enough to suggest
The capitol's dome, its patrician
Angle of shine.

And would it behoove us to render
A handful of heavy gray squares
For the temples of insurance?

(The man in the pinstriped suit nods *yes*.)
But embedded, please, in a swath of green
Balmy as Bushnell Park's.

What to do with the kid
Shot in the back last month by a cop
As the kid ditched a borrowed Caddy, a gun-

Shaped toy in his hand?
For weeks, the TV's photons
Have glowed his face, his serious eyes.

Is there room for the dead in this
Urban piece? Or at least
A rather slim, fresh-faced ghost?

A sawed-off moon-hunk is making its way up
From the suburbs to the east,
Home to the well-pruned hedge

And the brass-plated door. Let's make this collage
A night piece, a thin wash of moonlight
Holding us all lightly together:

Temples and cops,
Stripes and gold leaf, suburban hedge
And the beautiful

Dead kid whose eyes,
Whatever we brush over them,
Keep bleeding through.

In memory, Aquan Salmon (1986-2000)

Dream: Midwestern Motel

Semis hustle down the two-lane,
Chuffing oily smoke.

They'll be somewhere else by dark.
I've stopped early,

Taken by the lamps
Centered in each picture window,

The painted metal lawn chair
Placed by every door.

That's what you get for twenty-nine bucks,
And the pool, emptied last week.

Is it wind I hear, rustling lightly among
Those damp and crumbling walls,

Their blue
Faded quaintly as a fresco's?

Look—the sharp little stars of this place
Take up their posts in the sky.

They can't help their burning,
As I can't help my feeling small.

I lay myself on the swayback queen
That governs room number one-o-five,

My thoughts buffed blue
By Vacancy, its blinking sign.

From Grandview Terrace

A trash can bounces down Linnmoore Street,
Breasting the potholes deftly
As a bright round aluminum skiff.

I like the sound of it, the rattle and scrape
Of hollow on asphalt. What now, my sweet?

Touch me carefully,
I'm of the here and now,
Wired with the Dairy Mart's bad coffee
And the flux of our small burned-out city
Wherein forsythia have broached a subject
Too long unspoken of,

Which is to say,
The toothsome vagaries of yellow.

We're moving into a rank phase,
Can't you feel it?
The glare off windshields growing more astute,
The asphalt softening like butter,

The smog not smoky sweet, but heavier,
Pressing down like a lover who insists,
Who gets you going on that bus that you can't
Get off and finally don't want to.

Who knows what our lot will be by summer,
Whether these bushes stuck with tinfoil

Will seem festive then;
Ditto, the circulars from Sunday's paper,
Caught in the wind's steady thrusts?

Let trash festoon our *raison d'etre*.
Let the shades of a back-alley summer
Find us home.

Things, How They Need Us

Things, how they need us.

The clothes in the hamper, whimpering
To be pressed; the faucet
Disconsolate in its dripping;
The hedge, hungry for the saw.

    The things, the things, they cry out to us:

Paintings burdened with meaning,
Lines consigned to an obscure book.

They abide each other, the ear and the word,
The Alp and the heart
Aggrandized by its contemplation.

        To be a moon
        And not made into song,
        What kind of life
        Is that for a moon?

A stick, just a wooden thing
Until used to beat the prisoner
Shackled to a wall. The hand

Holding the stick, changes it then. The stick
And the hand enter history, flowing from them

    Like bad weather, like blood.

And who shall spare the things of the world
From us, we from them?

Flushed from their atomic houses,
Impaled on our names, neutrinos blink
In theory's glare.

          They must mourn
          Their lost privacy,
          These, our
          Littlest brothers,

Who stream through our bodies day and night,
Sequins of fear.

In the frail and crumbling structure
Of a kiss pressed to my mouth, I know
That we're not wise.

        Desire soils the earth.

But an earth unshaped by humanness,
What's that?

          Unsung rock,
          Lonely spinner
          Lost in its swaddle
          Of blue-green clouds.

To a Friend in Basque Country

Your e-mails come garnished with phrases
In that other tongue, and honey, it's bell-clear
You've been hooked, lined, and sinkered by a lingo
Not your own. Admit it, you're foraging
In a vocabulary studded
With words for the likes of a shepherd's shoe,
A slant of light, a passion I can't name,
Having no sound for a heat not quite lust
But a good deal warmer than affection.

You're quaffing new wine of which I only
Smell the fumes.
                         Once or twice, having tried
To speak aloud the phrases you've shipped,
I get a whiff of mountain air, hear brooks
Crash fluently over rocks. I expand,

Then fill again with the prim oxygen
Of Connecticut.

                         Why not visit? you write.
Why not? I reply, deeply wary
Of a province whose grammar, you've said, merges
Time and space, so the weeks that you've been gone
Become a gray room, its lonesome windows
Looking out to waves beating like hours.

Think of me, won't you? Back home, tending
To your old colloquial, keeping words
I hope you'll need again polished with use.

For E.M.

The Roses of Hartford

Summer's arrived,
The neighborhood grandiose with heat,
Sirens wailing at night, all night
Through open windows and doors.

Hell on earth, a woman says on the bus,
Mopping her face.

But it's hell gussied up with roses,
Tied to stakes, trained to wander the blank
Squares of trellises or to shade
The tenement's stoop. Bloom-heavy,
They stagger in place, red or yellow,
True to their load.

A bush of pink ones
Holds to the hill overlooking Pope Park
Where each day at noon, a dozen or more kids
Line up by the gate to the pool.

Through the chain-link fence,
Anyone can see the pool is dry.

And still the kids keep coming? you ask.

They do, their towels draped over backs
Glossy with sweat
As if any moment some streetwise angel
Might saunter to the spigot and twirl it,
Filling the cracked blue public space
With the long cold spill of plenitude.

Call City Hall, and they send you to Parks.
Call Parks, and they'll haw and hem.
By the time you're talking
To the mayor's office, you're hearing
That old saw in your head,

Don't you know
That the poor won't be saved, that this
Is not their kingdom?

There's hell on earth.

There are the roses' yellows,
And whites, and lavenders, and a red
So red you could weep.

Postmortem

Having stood at the edge of a hole dug
As depositary for the body,
I.e., the mortal bit, blip on the screen,
Form given to us, form taken;

                      having stood
Thus, and watched it lowered, the big box
Waxed and shined to a faux-bronze finish,

I've found words to be shyer than they seem.
Pushed to the edge, they won't leap. In the shade
Of the valley of death, they're toy lamps; they pierce
The wily darkness not. Still,

Bless the nouns and verbs of prayer, the hymnal's
Stodgy rhymes, vanishing in the careless sky
That roofs the bereaved—

                   any sound to efface
The syllable of wind jabbering in the ear,
And on fake metal, the thud of living rose.

Dream: Midwestern Lake Cabin

The loon, it grieves
On the lake. How does a loon grieve?

With quaking sound that shorts out high,
A goosed soprano.

The lake, it runs to the creek, there becoming
A fool over stones.

I nurse a fire at its edge.
Its flames make me look haunted,

My soul come back,
Stepping nimbly, like my mother

From her nap come to rouse me
From my own.

The moon, it croons
From the clouds. How so?

Delving into darkness, loosing beams
That hearten the pine beneath.

Moonlight is rarely
This brilliant, this young.

It knows itself in its crooning,
And the lake croons back,

Black circle sunk in a planet, with surface
For shine and burn.

The cabin stinks of propane.
Paths worn in the carpet take me

From bed to bath,
From couch to window to thoughts

Of what lives out there,
In the feral woods;

Of why the croppies
Won't bite after rain.

Lingua Franca

Staggering toward your mom and dad,
Ablaze with epiphany, *Yom frink schterm!*
You cried. We comprehended not.
You were a sea creature speaking
To the landed, a flame exhorting
The riffraff dark.

Child, it was a relief when you drifted
Into English, your single-footed hunks
Of Anglo-Saxon getting you
A bit of bread to gnaw, a toy, a kiss.

You'll have the rest in no time,
Greco-Latin roots and stems to ravish
Your cerebrum, a tad of French
For tasting the heart's passing *joie de vivre.*

Sweet as it was to give you milk
Warm from my body, to watch you,
A fat comma curled on me in sleep,

Nothing have I loved quite like this
Being at table with you,
Speaking of blizzards and androids,
November cranking the heat back on.

The old wind blows. Our tall house sways.
You look toward the window, turn,
A question in your eyes. What to say?

That first lovely, goofy
Lingo you spoke, did it have a word
For such as the solitude of cereal bowls,
Or how our sudden leaflessness
Denotes the morning's wintry shine?

Brief History of a Sentence

Let's start with the big picture:

The universe, i.e., great outward rush
Of fires and nights, and at its edge, among thickets of matter
Fraying, a star
Devolving into helium
And its sidekick, shine.

Which light
(Wave or particle? Music or poetry?) dashes
Through eons of miles until it impales our own
Blue-green wonder
Of continental drift, brokenhearted kin of the Hominidae.
You know the place.

Whereon stands (say it's a woman) a woman
On her porch, cold clear night in December, another autumn
Trashed. Let's pause
To mark our seasonal acquiescence to the powers
Of wind, the planet's dogged whirl. . . .

She draws her sweater close. The star punches its pinhole beam
Through the city's
Steady nerveless glow, arriving
Just as the woman—let's make her me—

Just as I look up,
A scintillating pebble sinking
Into my eye,
The retinal rods and cones
Honing the star to a hot
Potato of light tossed neuron to neuron.

And I, for a moment, a filament burning.

Under the power lines, among the sagging porches of my
Broken city, I am
Emerson on the Common, stoked
By the beyond, stowing for the universe
Its own erupted face.

Whereupon I make my sentence
For nothing and no one
But the rosebush my landlady tied
Sebastian-like to a stick
And cajoled into bloom; I say to that now defunct,
Thorned, stem-of-a-thing,

> *That's a star I haven't seen before.*

And the bush listens.

Afterword

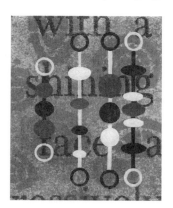

Rather plain, rather shy,
The period

Fixed to the end
Of a thought's luminous charge

Or a recipe's
Add flour and stir.

You stop.
You're a good reader,

Well trained.
You behave as you should.

Already, the mind is gunning
Toward the next

Capital looming, its serifs out
And flying, stiff as flags.

We fear
The bleached millionth of an acre

Between the noise of one sentence
And the noise of the next.

Words, our sisters
In fear, the flashlights we swing

Against the vacancy
That radiates without us,

Within. Don't get me wrong.
Nothing like Lingo

To deck out a silence,
Garnish a sigh.

But what word can guide us,
Virgil-like,

Through the silence
That springs fully formed

From the face
Of the dead beloved?

Look, my book
Has found its end, and rearing

Up,
Like the sudden,

Premonitory breathlessness
Of the body

Penetrated by a bullet
Or love—

Behold the Void
Before you and thrumming!

Whoa!
Why "Void"?

Why not
Re-name Vacancy

Room to breathe in,
To hold the heft

Of awe or grief?
As in a woods,

A clearing.

Notes

"My Mother Reads Me Lear's Alphabet": Edward Lear, the nineteenth-century British humorist, wrote many children's poems.

"The Diagrammer of Sentences": *In medio stat virtu,* "In the middle stands virtue," an observation attributed to Aristotle, among others; *In bocca chiusa.* . . , "The closed mouth gathers no flies," a Tuscan proverb.

"Father O.": *Hic est corpus meum;* "This is my body." In the New Testament, the words used by Jesus Christ at his last supper, as he blessed the bread and gave it to his disciples. The same words are used by the priest in the Roman Catholic mass at the moment of consecration when, for believers, the bread and wine become the body and blood of Christ.

"Homage to Mister Berryman": John Berryman jumped from a bridge over the Mississippi River in Minneapolis in January 1971.

"Midword": Quotations from and references to the following poems appear in these pages: John Berryman's "Dream Song I," Donald Justice's "Ode to Yellow," Elizabeth Bishop's "The Moose," Walt Whitman's "Song of Myself," and Jane Cooper's "The Flashboat."

"*from* Gods of the South End": The businesses whose names serve as section titles all are located in Hartford's South End. "Trinity" in "The Akropolis Market" refers to Trinity College, a small liberal arts institution in the same neighborhood.

About the Author

A native of Saint Paul, Clare Rossini is on the faculties of Trinity College in Hartford, Connecticut and the MFA in Creative Writing Program at Vermont College, Montpelier. Her poems have appeared in numerous journals and anthologies, including *The Kenyon Review, The Iowa Review, Poetry,* and *The Best American Poetry* series. She has received fellowships from the Connecticut Commission on the Arts, the Minnesota State Arts Board, and the Bush Foundation, and lives in West Hartford, Connecticut with her husband and son.